UNJUST:

WHEN BLACK AMERICANS ENCOUNTER THE UNITED STATES JUSTICE SYSTEM

DR. ANTHONY L. ROBBINS

UNJUST:

When Black Americans Encounter the United States Justice System

Dr. Anthony L. Robbins

Published by Pecan Tree Publishing
February 2022
Hollywood, FL
www.pecantreebooks.com

Paperback ISBN: 979-8-9855014-5-2
E-book ISBN: 979-8-9855014-6-9

Library of Congress Catalog Number: 2021902433

Cover Design by: Patricia Laurenceau Jean-Louis,
Laurenceau Design Studios
Interior Design by: Jenette Antonio Sityar
Interior Images: Licensed by Envato Elements

Pecan Tree Publishing
www.pecantreebooks.com

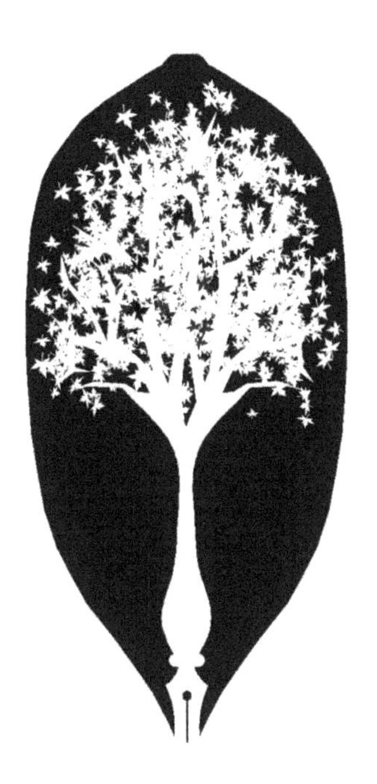

New Voices | New Styles | New Vision
Creating a New Legacy of Dynamic Authors and Titles
Hollywood, FL

ACKNOWLEDGMENTS

This book is dedicated to the known and unknown young men and women of color who have been victimized or discriminated against by the American justice system solely based on the color of their skin.

This book is dedicated to the fine young men and women of law enforcement who actually protect and serve by defending the rights of all people.

I dedicate this book to my mother, Seaner Robbins, an educator; and my father, Larry Robbins, Sr., a former member of the U.S. Department of Justice, Drug Enforcement Administration (Miami Field Office) for being so hard on me growing up. He taught me to evaluate life through unbiased eyes.

I dedicate this book to everyone that played a role in my life.

We must open our eyes and look at the true history of this great country and strive to make it better by accepting the fact that despite our historical trauma we have made excellent strides toward equality – yet – we still have a long way to go. Change starts within.

This book is not meant to promote racial bias, it's meant to educate America through the lens of an African American showing how the suppression of people of color is promoted and nurtured in America's legal and judicial systems. Ask yourself, if I place a knee on the side of your face can you honestly tell me what it feels like if you are the one applying the pressure?

This book is dedicated to those who consistently feel the weight of others maliciously applied in multiple areas of their lives – publicly and privately.

ABOUT THE AUTHOR

Having investigated thousands of criminal cases and having investigated over 200 Police misconduct cases involving race related discrimination and having successfully found evidence of discrimination and falsification of evidence in over 80% of the cases investigated, Miami based criminal defense investigator Anthony L Robbins, is the epitome of accomplishment, because of his overwhelming success as a criminal defense investigator in assisting to exonerate thousands of clients, Dr. Robbins has been introduced as one of the Top Criminal Defense Investigators in the nation.

Dr. Robbins specializes in complex criminal defense investigations and has been renowned for saving people form the death penalty and extensive jail time, Dr. Robbins specializes in Wrongful Conviction investigations, Police Misconduct and Race Motivated Discrimination. Dr. Robbins, the author of "Not Guilty - A Criminal Defense Investigator Guide to Wining your Case," is one of the few nationally recognized investigators who specialize in race motivated prosecution investigations.

Dr. Robbins, served as an active member of the City of Miami Community Relations Board as well as the City of Miami Civilian Investigative Panel who was tasked with investigating police misconduct allegations made against members of the City of Miami Police Department. Dr. Robbins was instrumental in ensuring that citizens were properly represented when filing complaints against law enforcement.

Dr. Robbins, has received specialized training in various fields which includes: Homicide Investigations with the Southern Police Institute, Ritualistic and Occult Crimes with the City of Sunrise Police Department Training Unit, Blood Spatter with the Miami-Dade Police Department Training Unit, and worked as a Special Best Interest Investigator with the Florida Guardian ad Litem Program, and on-going training to fight for minority families affected by the Social Service System.

Dr. Robbins' influence reaches beyond the South Florida community. He has investigated major cases across the United States. His demeanor garner respect from judges, prosecutors, and colleagues alike: as he has been honored by former U.S. President George W. Bush, former President Bill Clinton and received accommodations from two former Governors of the State of Florida as well as U.S. politicians.

TABLE OF CONTENTS

FOREWORD

It is an ugly and undeniable truth. America's Justice system is fundamentally flawed. Its major flaw is the racial disparity that permeates the criminal justice system. Dating back as early as 1915, Black men have often been portrayed as brutish, ignorant, prone to violence, and possessing a criminal nature, which perpetuates the belief that Black men are the poison of society. While it is true that the media is beginning to highlight Black individuals more positively, as a society, there is vast room for improvement.

The over-policing of Black communities leads to multiple arrests, which often result in plea-bargaining which, in turn, acts as a catalyst for mass incarceration. Innocent individuals often take a plea deal to avoid a lengthy jail or prison sentence. Because Black defendants are typically economically disadvantaged, they are not represented by an attorney or are assigned to a public defender who often has far too many cases to provide adequate and thorough representation. Thus, creating a pipeline to the mass incarceration of Black men and women.

Dr. Robbins, a trained law enforcement officer and criminal defense investigator (CDI), expertly explores the root causes of injustice through a historical lens that explains the patrolling and policing of Black people. He examines the way people of color are disproportionately targeted by law enforcement and its long-term effects on individuals and communities of color. Furthermore, he delves into the parallels of modern and historical police shootings and lynchings. Moreover, he offers insight into how we, as a society, can be a catalyst for systemic change.

S. Philip

INTRODUCTION

Love, money, pride, and ego; when investigating a major crime, most investigators can tie the motive back to these four factors. When investigating a crime, the police detective will act swiftly to determine which person closest to the victim may have had one of the aforementioned reasons for committing the felonious act. Additionally, police detectives weave together a story first, then they cast the actors-making sure to seek out those closest to the victim that fit the role perfectly. The detective does not concern themselves with whether or not the individual in question is truly innocent or guilty. Their goal is to close the file on their case as soon as possible.

We see this regularly on true crime television. Using the popular television series, *"The First 48"* as an example; the detectives immediately seek out to resolve the case within a predetermined period of time; and they look to do so by piecing together their own version of the story. Depending on an individuals' proximity to the victim; both physical and relationship; an innocent person may end up finding themselves on the wrong side of the interrogation table.

In addition to hiring an attorney right away, it is most important to make sure that the attorney has a capable and experienced CDI at their disposal. Police investigations tend to be flawed, and a skilled CDI will work diligently to uncover each and every one of them.

In my first book, *Not Guilty: A Criminal Defense Investigator's Guide to Winning Your Case,* I laid out the way in which police detectives seek to close cases easily without doing their proper due diligence. In this book, my goal is to address the way in which people of color tend to fit the profile more often than not. As both a trained law enforcement officer and a CDI, I can speak to how often Black people-specifically Black men "fit the profile" of a suspect. Even when the details in the BOLO (be on the lookout) specifically give details about the individual in question, law enforcement officers offer few, if any, apologies when they harass, arrest, or worse-the wrong individual.

Dr. Anthony L. Robbins

CHAPTER

Fitting the Profile

In May of 2019, law enforcement officers in Los Angeles, California forcibly arrested a Black man while they were responding to a domestic violence call. The dispatcher had yet to give a description of the suspect, but the officers saw a Black man and determined that he was the violator they were looking for. Audio from the officers reveals that upon seeing a Black man, one officer asked the other if that was the "dude" they were looking for. The other responded "probably." With that, the Black "dude" was arrested for being in the proximity of where the domestic violence occurred. As it turns out, the person they should have been looking for was a White man. The woman who made the 911 call tried to tell the officers that they had the wrong man; however, the officers arrived at the scene to make an arrest, and they were determined to do so, even if it meant arresting the wrong person. Too often, that wrong person happens to be a person of color.

It is common for people of color to automatically be assumed guilty-often with no factual basis for the assumption. There have been instances when law enforcement officers have arrested individuals of color even when they have on the spot knowledge that the person has done nothing wrong; for instance, like in the cases mentioned above where the victim or 911 caller is present and tells the responding officers that they have their handcuffs or guns drawn on the wrong person.

These situations can be reasoned away by bad judgment or human error. However, there have been instances where law enforcement officers have knowingly arrested innocent Black people.

In 2013 and 2014, a small police department in Miami, Florida intentionally sought out to present their town as a safe place with a very capable police department. After burglaries occurred within the town of Biscayne Park, Florida-the *then* chief of police decided that he wanted to show a 100% clearance rate. This meant that every one of those cases needed to show that an arrest had been made. Having a 100% clearance rate on crimes within their jurisdiction is the dream of every law enforcement agency, but this is not a likely outcome; so of course, it was noticeable when Biscayne Park police department managed to do so.

Raimundo Atesiano was the chief of police at that time and had instructed his officers to clear these cases by any means necessary. Atesiano had the idea to have his officers detain random Black people who had the audacity to drive their car or walk through their small town. The officers were told to run a check on the individual, and if they had any type of record, they were to arrest them for one of the burglaries.

Both the arresting officers and the chief were aware that the individuals were randomly chosen to take the wrap for these crimes, and they knew that the people were innocent. In one particular case, Atesiano and his officers framed an innocent 16-year-old for four burglaries in their city and in another case, an innocent Black man was framed, arrested, and charged with five different burglaries that occurred in one day.

This case came to light after several police officers sent anonymous letters to the city manager, alerting the manager to the fact that the chief had asked the officers to target innocent Black men. Although these Black men were wrongfully targeted, the arrest tarnished them and had long-term impact.

The way in which people of color are disproportionately targeted by law enforcement officers does not just impact the aforementioned. Researchers like Harvards' David R. Williams have found that news of police attacks against Blacks weighs emotionally and mentally on other blacks within the community.

A study done by Harvard University in October 2016 (Rage, Racism and Health: Challenges and Opportunities) found that when police killings happen within a Black community, it impacts the success rate of Black students within that community. The adverse effect on their performance is even higher when the victim is unarmed.

Minority communities are overpoliced and their presence does not make residents feel safer--in fact, it makes them feel more fearful. This feeling of "protect and serve" does not seem to exist within the Black community. The police represent a sense of safety in certain communities, but in Black communities, they are a source of stress and strife.

The justice system continually fails victims of police brutality and murders. More often than not, when a case is presented to the judicial system prosecutors fail to react and if they do decide to pursue charges, there is often a failure to convict. This lack of justice further victimizes both the direct victims, their families, and the surrounding communities. Additionally, due to these historic failures, members of the Black community tend to not only feel unsafe in the presence of law enforcement officers; there is this sense that the justice system is as prejudice as the police.

Members of the Black community are left with a feeling of being highly visible in terms of being targeted by the police, and invisible when seeking justice.

Love, money, pride, and ego may account for the cause of most major crimes that occur, but I will add that a system of racism in America has been the cause of crimes committed against Black America at the hands of an unjust system of justice.

CHAPTER

The Black Image

T*he First 48* is not just a catchy name for a reality show about crime solving; it depicts an accurate amount of crucial time in solving a felony case-specifically murder. The question then becomes whether or not law enforcement officers are actually interested in solving cases or clearing them.

The unlawful case that came to light in Biscayne Park, Florida should not be thought of as exclusive. It may have been unique in that specific orders were given by the chief of police; but even in situations where the police chief may be law-abiding, there are still law enforcement officers that are spoiled fruit. Based on what we know about racial profiling, it is not a difficult assertion to make that law enforcement officers may unlawfully target Black citizens in order to give a false sense of protecting the community and solving crimes.

Unfortunately, Black men have long been portrayed as the disease that plagues society. Images strewn throughout the media; news, movies, and television shows-support the belief that the Black man and the boogey man are the same. Stereotypical images of Black men on television are so common, we have become desensitized because of it. These portrayals of the big bad Black man date back as early as 1915 when the film "Birth of a Nation" premiered. The purpose of the film was to show that the Black man was one to be feared and the White man-including ones in white robes and hoods, were the ones that would save the country from them.

These negative images do not just date back to the early 1900s. The 1970s and 80s continued this myth by parading Black men in handcuffs on the nightly news, making anyone who watched believe that Black men were the poison of society and White men with guns and handcuffs were the cure.

In recent years, the media has tried to erase the sins of its past. It has become more common to see positive images of Black people on television, but the damage is done and repairing it could take generations. In the meantime, Black men are being systematically and unfairly targeted-being arrested for something that would result in a warning for a White man; charged with crimes they may not have committed and subjected to an unfair system of justice. The court system that touts itself as blind, does not seem to be colorblind.

As of 2018, Black men made up about 13% of the male population in the United States, but about 35% of incarcerated men in the U.S. prison system. This disproportionate rate speaks to a system that is anything but colorblind. What makes this system of justice so undignified is that the policies and crime-based laws are targeted toward Black and disadvantaged communities.

The over-policing of Black and disadvantaged communities leads to arrests for absurd types of crimes, and this then leads to an unfair plea-bargaining system and mass incarceration. Plea-bargains are a tool that the judicial system uses against those who are not represented by an attorney or those who are being represented by an overloaded public defender. Innocent Black people often take a plea deal in order to avoid a lengthy jail or prison sentence. They are led to believe that the charges against them will lead to a guilty verdict if taken to trial. The plea bargain leads to mass incarceration of Black men (and women).

Mass incarceration speaks to the way in which the United States imprisons people at high and ever-increasing rates. According to the Brennan Center of Justice. from 1970 to the mid-2000s, the prison population in America increased by about 700%. The U.S. has the highest rate of prisoners per capita than any other country. This is not by accident. The 13th Amendment of the United States Constitution prohibits slavery, with one exception, prisoners.

After the Civil War and the freeing of slaves, a ton of targeted laws went into effect. These laws were extremely specific to behaviors and patterns that were known to be common to Black people and most common amongst Black men. These laws made legal behaviors illegal, which then gave the police the right to arrest and incarcerate those who violated them. Vagrancy, loitering, sitting down in the front seats of a bus, drinking from a water fountain when thirsty, and exercising free speech rights. The authorities could not make being Black illegal, so they found loopholes.

Once these Black people were arrested, they were quickly placed before the courts and convicted. They could then be placed into jails or prisons for an absurd amount of time where they became "property" once again. The 13th Amendment provided a loophole which allowed states to force these people to work for free once again. Where slavery was prohibited, the 13th Amendment loophole provided Black men as slaves once again.

Unfortunately, the way in which Black people have been treated in the United States is not just a matter for the history books. This mistreatment falls under "current affairs." The examples of police misconduct mentioned previously are just a pebble being tossed in the ocean. These stories are far too common within the Black community and those in the position to make changes have been operating as if they have blinders on.

There is an urgency to have Black and brown people in the rooms where policies are being created. America has a racism problem, and this can only be addressed with honesty and transparency, and by having diversity at the top levels of criminal justice organizations.

At this point Blacks in America are socially and economically disadvantaged and there has been a heavy weight placed on our shoulders. There is an expectation that when we go outside, we do not appear angry and hostile toward an America that has treated us with anger and hostility. It is time that we take a serious look at the state if Black Americans and how we have been severely impacted by societal constructs. Because of my role as a defense investigator, I am placing a strong emphasis on the way the criminal justice system has violated Black America, but we cannot be limited in our knowledge that the problem exists outside of the justice system. Although our focus here is mostly within the justice system, we must open our eyes to the way systemic racism has infiltrated all the veins of society. However, because the criminal justice system deals in life-or-death scenarios; not just quality of life, there needs to be a sense of urgency when addressing with this problem.

The criminal justice system and the way in which it operates today is like a cancer that is running rampant within communities of color. We are tasked with finding a cure.

CHAPTER

I CAN'T BREATHE
BLM
BLACK
LIVES
MATTER
NO JUSTIC
NO PEACE

America, We Have a Problem

America has a racism problem.

There are some who will readily dispute this for varied reasons. There might be some who are naïve in thinking that America's racism problem was cured on November 4, 2008, when Barack Obama was elected the 44th President of the United States. There were many who believed that a racist country could not elect a Black president, so therefore America could not be racist any longer, right?

Then there are some who like to say they are colorblind and do not see color and therefore they filter everything through that lens. When a problem occurs, they assume that the issue is anything other than color. When an unarmed Black man is shot, colorblind folks say comments like "they were shot because they did not comply with the officer, not because of their skin color."

Then of course there are those who due to ignorance and bigotry, cannot see the issue with their racism and in fact believe that the police are well within their right when involved in the killing and brutality of unarmed Black people and people of color. Just like those who are colorblind, they feel that Black people should be more compliant, but further to that, they feel that the police are almost always (if not always) justified in their actions.

We will always have people who fall into these categories, so for the rest of us, we are tasked with finding the cure for this disease that has infested Black America for far too long. History books need to be rewritten so that they tell the true story of America, even the ugly parts. Critical Race Theory needs to be part of the K-12 Curriculum and should be required as core classes for college students. As it stands right now, foreign language is required in some school districts in order to graduate high school yet, understanding the plight of our own underserved citizens is being voted out and is considered too sensitive of a topic to cover.

America has a racism problem and ignoring it or pretending it away is not the cure. We must look at this situation head on and tackle this issue. Too many lives have been taken in vain and too many have fallen victim to an unjust system of justice. By the time the name of a client reaches my desk, it is too late. They have already been victimized by unfair accusations and I am tasked with shining light in the dark corners of a system filled with human rodents.

So often, I am tasked with uncovering truths about criminal cases because law enforcement officers assumed guilt and did not thoroughly investigate. There is no way to say for sure that the reasons are biased, but when so many of the victims of injustice are Black or people of color, it is difficult to not have those feelings.

Racism against Black people and people of color is built into the foundation of this country -- From the moment immigrants landed on this soil and began to brutalize the Natives of this land, through the enslavement of people from Africa, through the aftermath of slavery which includes Jim Crow laws, legalized lynching of people of color, and a system of justice which furthers the brutality.

There are numerous ways in which the criminal justice system brutalizes Black people and people of color; however, let's start with the brutality that takes place at the street level.

Police brutality, according to Amnesty International, is the excessive use of force by a police officer that goes beyond what is necessary to control the situation to which they are responding. What is unfortunate is that many times, these situations would only call for a traffic citation or a warning. This causes anger and frustration within disadvantaged communities and people of color. A traffic stop for most people can be an inconvenience. For a Black person, it can be stressful, elevate anxiety and in some cases feel like a life-or-death situation.

To be fair, most police involved stops do not involve violence, and this is across the board without regard to race. Unfortunately, when violence is involved, it is disproportionately involving Black people or people of color.

From my experience as a law enforcement officer, I can attest that mental health issues either pre-dating the job or caused by job stressors is real. Police work is mostly mundane if you can believe that, but when things do go wrong, they go wrong quickly and usually without warning. These on-the-job stressors can cause police officers to respond in a way that is called a "startle response." This response is usually what occurred when you hear an officer say, "I thought I saw a gun" or something along that manner. This is similar to what officer Jeronimo Yanez used as a defense to his fatal shooting of Philando Castile in 2016. This defense is part of what Yanez and his attorneys used. The officer said that he was reacting to the actions of Castile.

In the case of Philando Castile, he had a permit to carry a concealed weapon and notified the officer as he was supposed to do. In other cases, the victim was not armed at all, yet still police officers will use the startle response as a defense. Understand that a regular citizen, under similar circumstances, could be convicted of a crime if they use deadly force when startled, but a trained officer of the law can use this as a legal defense, and the courts often justify this defense with a "not guilty" verdict. Some of these cases however never see the inside of a court room and often just result in a temporary paid administrative leave.

Too often, the startle response results in the disproportionate killing of an unarmed Black person and the justice system does not always respond appropriately.

CHAPTER

How
Many
Weren't
Filmed
#BLM

The Effectiveness of the Black Lives Matter Movement

The Black Lives Matter (BLM) movement was formed in the United States in 2013. The goal was to shine a spotlight of the way in which Black people are targeted for violence at the hands of White people, due to implicit bias. Subsequently, it was also used in response to police brutality and the way in which it disproportionately impacts the Black community. Through both written and expressed protests, BLM is dedicated to fighting racism and anti-Black violence, especially as it relates to the brutal way in which the police encounter Black folks. One belief that drives this movement is that Black people within the United States are far more likely to be brutalized or unjustly killed by law enforcement officers than White people.

Although the BLM movement began in 2013, it gained attention in 2014 after the police involved murder of Michael Brown in Ferguson, Missouri. The murder of Brown, who was unarmed, propelled BLM onto the national stage.

Research done by Travis Campbell published in May 2021 in the SSRN-Elsevier Journal revealed that during 2014 and 2019, there was a decrease in police homicides which resulted in 300 fewer deaths. Campbell credits the movement and the protesting of police violence as the cause of this decrease. Campbell found that in cities where protests were large or frequent, this is where the larger decreases occurred.

The use of social media and viral videos is also instrumental to our increase in knowledge about brutal force by law enforcement officers. Police violence against disadvantaged members of society are not new, but more light has been shone and this places pressure on law enforcement agencies to take a look at their systems.

Where we have seen a decrease in police violence due to the BLM efforts, it has shown little effectiveness in the courts. This does not mean that progress has not been made.

Former Dallas police officer Amber Guyger was convicted of killing Botham Jean, an unarmed Black man who was sitting on his sofa eating. She had entered his apartment in September of 2018 and shot him. Her defense was that she thought she was in her own apartment, and he was a burglar.

In 2017, Michigan State Trooper used a taser on Damon Grimes during a police chase and the use of the taser caused the teenager to crash his all-terrain vehicle (ATV) which resulted in his death. The trooper was convicted of involuntary manslaughter.

The Chicago police officer that shot Laquan McDonald in the back in 2014, was convicted of second-degree murder and a series of other offenses.

More recently, Derek Chauvin was convicted for the 2020 murder of George Floyd. A murder that was witnessed across the world due to the video that was captured by Darnella Frazier. It is worth noting that Ms. Frazier won a Pulitzer Prize citation for her capture.

In the past, protests and riots have taken place due to the lack of conviction regarding brutality against Blacks at the hands of law enforcement officers.

In 1980, a race riot took place in Miami, Florida due to the courts' failure to convict the four police officers who brutally beat to death Arthur McDuffie after a traffic stop.

In 1992, Los Angeles had riots due to the courts' lack of conviction after the beating of Rodney King by four police officers and also a slap on the wrist for the murder of Latasha Harlins at the hands of a Korean store owner.

Although at the time of this writing, published research and findings have not caught up with recent court convictions, but in taking an educated guess I would imagine that the BLM movement has had profound impact on these positive outcomes.

One way in which we have seen truly insignificant impact is policy. The way current law enforcement policies are written allows for brutality without consequence. This is why even when the evidence shows that the brutality was unnecessary, police officers maintain their employment, or are hired by other departments almost immediately after losing employment due to brutality.

Although the BLM movement has had minor impact over current policy, there has been more attention paid to the need for police reform and changes in policy because of it.

In 2019, in the Proceedings of the National Academy of Sciences of the United States of America (PNAS), Frank Edwards, Hedwig Lee and Michael Esposito did a study to look at the risk of being killed by police use of force in the United States. In their research they found that one in every 1,000 Black men should expect to be killed by the police and that Black women and men as well Native men and women are more likely to be killed by the police than their White counterparts. However, among all the groups, Black men and women are more likely to be killed by the police than other at-risk groups.

Recent events have shown us that an armed and dangerous White man is more likely to be treated with humanity by the police than an unarmed Black man.

Jeffrey Nicolas killed two sheriff deputies; however, he was arrested unharmed by police. Murder suspect Peter Manfredonia was taken into custody by police unharmed. Roger Hedgpeth was arrested unharmed, after threatening to kill a sitting president. Benjamin Murdy fired 200 rounds at police and the police did not fire a single shot back. Not one! He was arrested unharmed. Jerri

Kelly held a gun on four Black high school teenagers who knocked on her door while fund-raising. The police arrived to find the four Black students lying on the ground at gun point. They waited five days to arrest her, and she was not harmed.

The list of White, armed, and dangerous people that have been arrested unharmed by the police goes on and on and could fill the pages of this book.

The differences between Black police encounters and White police encounters seems clear. America has a racism problem, and this problem is built into our foundation.

White Americans sailed to the continent of Africa, violently kidnapped Black people, shackled them, and carried them like cargo to the United States. The descendants of those White Americans has the audacity to refer to the descendants of their cargo as savages and then treats them as such.

Black people in America have been mistreated (to put it mildly) since those vessels anchored off the shores of Africa and the problem persists even till today. Police violence against people of color is not a new issue, it is actually at the core of policing in America.

CHAPTER

Policing - A Historical Perspective

College textbooks like to refer to Sir Robert Peel as the father of modern democratic policing. Peel created the Metropolitan Police in London, England in 1829 and he designed them with the purpose of maintaining safety and security within communities.

According to the United States Department of Justice (ojp.gov), Peel proposed nine principles under which the police would operate:

To prevent crime and disorder; to perform their duties upon public approval of police actions; secure and maintain respect of the public; the understanding that the use of physical force could diminish cooperation from the public; absolute impartial service to the laws; to only use physical force to the extent of what is necessary to restore order and only after warnings were found to be insufficient; to maintain a relationship with the public; to not usurp (take illegally or by force) the powers of the judiciary, and finally that they would be evaluated by the absence of crime and disorder.

When I started my criminal justice studies, what I learned were the ideals about policing in America, in reality the truths about American policing are quite ugly. Although college textbooks like to tell the story of Sir Robert Peel as the foundation of policing in America, the true foundation lies in the institution of slavery.

Dr. Victor E. Kappeler did a study about the history of American policing and its ties to slavery *(A Brief History of Slavery and the Origins of American Policing, January 7, 2014)*. Police in America were formed in order to capture runaway slaves and control minorities. What was once slave patrols and White night watchmen are now what we call uniformed police in America. Police, formerly known as slave patrols, helped maintain economic order by helping slave owners capture and punish runaway slaves.

This patrolling of minorities continued even after slavery ended and the police were used to enforce color laws and punish Black folks that broke those laws. Many of the lynchings that took place in America, happened under the watch of police. Although our history books like to make it appear as if lynchings were a thing that occurred because citizens took the law into their own hands; the reality is that it was actually done under the pretext of law and justice.

According to the NAACP (National Association for the Advancement of Colored People), "a lynching is the public killing of an individual who has not received any due process." Does this sound familiar? The NAACP goes on to say that "lynchings were violent public acts that White people used to terrorize and control Black people..." Lynchings were considered a celebration of White supremacy and photos of lynchings were often the backdrop of postcards.

Historically, growing up Black in the American South meant living under the constant threat of being lynched. This act of terror was used to control people of color and make them act in accordance with the laws set forth by White men. In his book *Black Boy,* Black author Richard Wright wrote about how his conduct was controlled by the knowledge of lynchings. He was indirectly impacted by these acts of terror because he knew people that had been victims of lynching.

Lynchings were acts of terror that was used for the punishment of a broad range of *crimes*. Black men were lynched for looking at White women; associating with White women; having a physical altercation with a White man; accusations of raping a White woman (without proof) and often later found to be untrue. Unfortunately, by the time it was found to be untrue, the lynching had already taken place. In my studies, I have yet to come across stories about the regret of those involved in these false accusations.

Many of the lynchings that took place were against successful Black people and it is believed that it was done so to suppress Black success. These crimes of terror were not limited to people who had been accused of crimes-real or imagined.

In March of 1901 in Rome, Tennessee, a Black man reportedly found a wallet and kept the money that was in it. William Crutchfield was arrested by the authorities. That night, a White mob came into the jail to take him and lynch him. Just as he was about to be lynched, he broke free and escaped. The White men who had gathered to lynch him became angry and went searching for him. When they went looking for him, they could not find him so instead they found his sister, Ballie Crutchfield in her home.

In order to quench their thirst for Black blood, the angry White mob took Ballie Crutchfield as a substitute for her brother, took her to a bridge, shot her in the head and threw her body into the water below them. Her body was found the next day and the coroner concluded that her death was at the hands of unknown parties.

No one was held accountable for the murder of Ballie Crutchfield.

CHAPTER

Modern Day Lynching

When looking at the current state of affairs as it relates to the police shootings of unarmed Black men, it is hard to not draw a parallel between these shootings and historical lynchings.

When we look at the NAACP's definition of lynching, "public killing of an individual who has not received any due process," it is synonymous with what we are witnessing currently. Police murder unarmed Black men and women in public, often captured on police body cameras or very often captured by cell phone cameras of someone standing nearby.

The reasoning given by law enforcement is often the same; the person did not comply with authorities, or the armed and para-military trained police officer felt threatened by the unarmed Black person. Oftentimes, just like in the case of Ballie Crutchfield, no one is held responsible for the murders, even when it is clear who pulled the trigger.

Further, regardless of the reason given by law enforcement agencies, when a police officer uses deadly force on an unarmed person, they have acted as if they are the totality of the justice system and have decided both guilt and punishment-often within seconds of approaching their victim.

Just like in the historical cases, modern day lynchings are not just being done at the hands of law enforcement officers. In 2020, a father and son in Glynn Count, Georgia decided that Ahmaud Arbery had burglarized homes (although there were no known burglaries) and they determined justice. Even if Ahmaud Arbery had committed the crime they had accused him of, the penalty for that crime was not death. When they chased the jogger in their truck and executed him, they were initially not punished. It was not until word of the lynching spread across social media and media outlets, that justice was sought. Later, a friend of the lynch mob released a video he had captured of the lynching.

Prior to the lynching of Ahmaud Arbery, police in Louisville, Kentucky shot and killed Breonna Taylor while she was asleep in her bed. Justice has not been served as of yet, and in fact, the authorities have found a way to justify the murder of the sleeping woman.

Using the word "lynching" to describe the crimes against unarmed Black people makes a lot of people uncomfortable. It evokes anger and hurt in some people of color but for others, it evokes guilt and shame. There is a desire from some people to be disconnected from the sins of their ancestors; however, in order to gain a full understanding of the terror and horror involved in these crimes, we must look at it from this perspective.

The United States House of Representatives Resolution, H.R. 35, commonly known as the anti-lynching bill was passed the House in February 2020. The law which would punish hate crimes at a federal level, has been delayed by the Senate. As of the date if this writing, lynching in the United States is not a federal crime. The Senate, which is historically a good ole' boys club, is not motivated to make the unlawful killing of Black people a federal crime.

CHAPTER

STOP RACISM
RIOT NOW
MAKE IT STOP

Police Oversight and Local Policies

A lack of movement at the federal level leaves local municipalities tasked with protecting all citizens from rogue police officers. Civilian Oversight Boards are one resource that local agencies can use to help with this issue.

Civilian Oversight Boards can go by different names in different communities, but the bottom line is the same; non-police officers looking into police activity without the bias that wearing a badge can bring. These boards normally operate independently of the police and other local officials and designed to investigate police misconduct.

In order for these boards to be effective, there must be proper funding, resources, and autonomy. Additionally, it is important that these civilian boards represent the demographics of the community. As it stands right now, most boards make recommendations about disciplinary actions that should be brought against police officers, however the department heads have the final say, and too often, after an administrative leave or disciplinary action the officer is placed back on the job without consequence.

In order to be effective, civilian boards should follow the investigator-focused model in order to be better equipped to deal with police accountability. This board should consist of civilians who are educated in the field of law, policy making and other focused expertise that would allow them the knowledge and skills necessary to make educated decisions on a matter and then have the authority to discipline the officers or recommend discipline that department leaders will have to enforce. Having police who police their own historically results in bad actors being placed back on the street to inflict more harm on society.

As it stands right now, the majority of law enforcement agencies have civilian boards that follow a review-focused model rather than the investigator-focused model. These boards are usually staffed by members of the community who have been appointed by municipality leaders. The problem with this is that the boards can be stacked based on political views and affiliations which could lead to bias. This is counterproductive. The way in which civilian boards are manned should be based on qualifications and experience, not relationships with mayors and commissioners.

Members of the Black community are severely impacted by faulty police work and policies and therefore they should be represented on civilian review boards. There needs to be Black people and people of color represented in the places where decisions are being made that impact Black people.

When people of color are not seated in the board rooms of policy making organizations, this can result in Black folks falling victim to "race-neutral" policies.

Race-Neutral policies are what occur when policy makers fail to realize the impact their decisions have on Black people or other disadvantaged members of society. Policy makers make these decisions and pretend to not know the implicit bias involved in them.

A notable example of race-neutral policies is the difference between the penalties for possessing crack rather than the more expensive cocaine. It is believed that more affluent people use cocaine, while poor Black people use crack. By making the penalties for using crack more severe than cocaine, it targets and criminalizes a specific part of society. What makes these policies "race-neutral" is that unlike the "drinking from a whites-only water fountain" or "sitting in the front of the bus" was clear and targeted; whereas making crack possession more of a crime, does not exclude any race from being penalized, but those making the laws know that the drug is used more by one group than another. By doing this, they can say that the policy is not about race, although it clearly is.

This is why it is important that Black people must take a more active role in the politics taking place with their community and in society as a whole. Black people are more apt to not get involved in these matters, but they are most impacted by them.

CHAPTER

NLY ONE RACE
HUMAN RACE
BLACK LIVES
MATTER
MY
CO
NOT

The Race Gap in Law Enforcement

Research done by the Pew Research Center (The Racial Confidence Gap in Police Performance, 2016) found that whites had a more positive view of the police than their Black counterparts. According to the research Whites believe that the deaths of Blacks at the hands of police officers are isolated events, where Black people feel that the events are based on a larger societal problem. The research also showed that less than 15% of Blacks had confidence in their local police departments to protect them.

In my experience, Black people are less likely to call the police to report an incident against them, because they fear that the police will come and further victimize them. Their feelings are not baseless.

James Smith of Fort Worth, Texas has said that he lives with the guilt associated with the death of his neighbor Atatiana Jefferson. It was Mr. Smith who called the police to check on the welfare of his neighbor when he saw her door open in the middle of the night. The police arrived and Ms. Jefferson heard noise outside her window, grabbed her gun and that is when the officer shot and killed her through her window. The police were called to check on Ms. Jefferson, yet she ended up being victimized by them.

In another incident in Los Angeles County, three teenagers (two of which were Black), were attacked by a White homeless man. A bystander called the police to report the attack and the police ended up holding the victims at gunpoint. The bystanders who called the police were pleading with the police and attempting to let them know that the teens were victims. The bystanders reported that the police were unresponsive to hearing the truth.

In Rochester, New York, the police were called after the parents reported their nine-year-old as experiencing a mental crisis. In response to the nine-year-old's actions, the police pepper sprayed her, handcuffed her, and placed her in the back of the police car. As the child pleaded for help, the police officer is heard on the body camera saying, "you did it to yourself, hon."

What remains problematic when addressing the views and experiences of whites over blacks is this; police departments overwhelmingly do not look like the demographics of the communities they service. More often than not, non-Black police officers are patrolling Black communities.

In the 2015 article titled "The Political Context of the Percent Black-Neighborhood Violence Link: A Multilevel Analysis",

Criminologist Maria Velez found that crime rates in minority neighborhoods were lower when the demographics of the police department matched the community. When the police look like the people they serve, it not only helps the officers to understand the culture better, but it also changes the way in which the community interacts with and responds to the police.

When speaking with my clients or members of the community, one thing I have noticed in reference to this topic, is that Black people have increased anxiety when approached by a White police officer, and extraordinarily little to no anxiety when the police officer looks like them. Not to say that the culture of policing does not have an impact on how Black police officers act, but the perspective of the community is drastically different when dealing with one of their own.

While some law enforcement agencies are attempting to hire diverse groups, the reality is that a career in law enforcement does not naturally appeal to many people of color. Where many obviously see a career in law enforcement as a good thing, there are more who see police officers as their natural enemy, and this makes it more difficult for them to see it as a viable career.

Jack Glaser, PhD, a social psychologist has stated that it is "not productive to demonize police." (Policing in Black & White, 2016). Glaser believes that police departments are eagerly seeking solutions to reduce racial disparities. These solutions are based on studies that were done by the National Bureau of Economic

Research, 2016 and the Center for Policing Equity, 2016. The studies titled "An Empirical Analysis of Racial Differences in Police Use of Force", found that Black people are not more likely to commit crimes, they are however more likely to encounter police.

Data analyzed by Jennifer Eberhardt, PhD and published in Stanford News, June 15, 2016, written by Clifton B. Parker found that although Black residents accounted for only 28% of the population (as of 2016) of Oakland, California, they accounted for 60% of police stops. It was also found that Black men are more likely to be searched during a traffic stop than White men. It is worth noting that Philando Castile was pulled over for having a broken taillight. That routine traffic stop ended in the lynching of Mr. Castile and no accountability for the officer that killed him.

Law enforcement agencies need to address the racial gaps within their departments and find solutions for their demographic disparities. Current research uses Michael Brown and Ferguson, Missouri as the starting point for conversation on race and policing. The use of hashtags and the viral nature of the BLM amplified the conversation. Policing agencies can no longer ignore the conversations and in fact, they must take an active role in the dialogue.

It is way too late in the conversation to say that law enforcement agencies must be proactive in their approach. So much damage has been done-but they must immediately act and get at the front of finding immediate solutions. One way to do this is to have more people of color in high-ranking positions in their departments; another approach is to immediately get out into disadvantaged communities and recruit starting as early as middle school. Another way is to start promoting programs like the Police Athletic League (PAL) and Police Explorer programs. These are ways to change the perspective that Black youths have toward law enforcement and get them excited about a career in the field.

CHAPTER

Engaging Black Youth

Recently a community in Michigan restarted their PAL program after taking time off due to COVID-19. Chief Vernon Coakley of the Kalamazoo Department of Public Safety said in a report done by Lexie Petrovic on June 17, 2021 and published on wwmt.com that he is using this program as an opportunity for community outreach. The purpose of PAL in places like Kalamazoo as well as other U.S. cities is to have an early and positive impact on youth from disadvantaged communities. It is a way that the police can change the way youth view them and interact with them. It can also be used as a way to build early interest in the law enforcement field. Chief Coakley credits PAL for shaping his life as a child, growing up in Detroit, Michigan.

Studies like the one by Corliss Bean and Tanya Forneris in 2014 titled "Participants' experiences of the Police Athletic League: Using sport as a vehicle to positive youth development" done in reference to the effectiveness of PAL have shown that the respect young people gain for police officers in social situations can impact the way they respond to them when they are on the job and would potentially have a healthy respect for the law.

Another means of engaging disadvantaged is the police explorer program. These programs are community based and purposed with engaging with youth and nurturing a passion for a law enforcement career.

Youth can get involved in the police explorer programs as early as middle school and can remain involved into early adulthood. The program is designed to build awareness of how the criminal justice system works, developing character, promoting a respect for the rule of law, maintaining good physical fitness, and promoting responsible citizenship.

Programs like this can be effective in engaging disadvantaged youth and giving them the opportunity to garner interest in a law enforcement career. This type of engagement with Black youth can begin the process of closing the racial gaps that are apparent in many law enforcement agencies across the U.S. and take meaningful steps toward healing the wounds that currently exist.

Another effective means of engaging with disadvantaged youth is through community policing. Community policing is not a new idea, but it has always felt more like an ideal than anything realistic. The purpose of community policing is to build a foundation of trust within a community between that communities' residents and police.

Community policing does require trust which is something that the police are tasked with establishing. The community also has to play a significant role as well. No relationship can flourish if it is strictly one-sided. The police have to be present in the community, not just in response to an incident. The community has to be receptive.

Programs like PAL and the police explorer programs can have nominal fees attached and although those fees might be considered small, they might still be more than a family can afford. Community policing, and the activities that go along with it can be a way that youth, as well as their parents and guardians can connect with their local law enforcement officers without incurring cost.

Community policing works. Seeing police officers interacting with local residents; having sidewalk conversations; pickup basketball games; street football and other informal methods can build foundations of trust. This type of trust is essential in creating a relationship between the police and the Black community. This is always another way of garnering interest in a law enforcement career for youth who have a soured impression of police.

CHAPTER

END
POLICE
BRUTALITY
NOW
Justice
GEORGE
FLOYD
1st degree
Chauvin

The High Cost of Police Brutality Against the Black Community

Police brutality comes at a cost. Very seldom is the price paid by the officer or officers involved. When there is a civil penalty to pay, the funds come from tax dollars paid by private citizens. However, the full cost of police brutality (on top of the unnecessary loss of life) is the mental health impact it causes.

Over the last few years, dozens of research studies have been done to address the mental impact that police brutality against Black folks has on other Black folks. Even when the victim was unknown to another person, that other person has a mental and emotional response.

A study done in 2018 by Atheendar S. Venkataramani and published by The Lancet (Police Killings and their spillover effects on the mental health of Black Americans) found that "police killings of unarmed African Americans have adverse effects on mental health among Black American adults who were not directly affected by the incident." It is worth noting that the impact was even more dangerous for Black middle school and high school youth. The impact is stronger for Black citizens who reside in the community where the brutality or subsequent murder took place.

Younger youth are impacted in a unique way. They see the videos (unfortunately) and are left confused by them. Historically, children from all ethnic backgrounds were taught that the police protect us. That conversation has begun to change in many homes, but this is the theory most primary schools still teach. When these younger children see this viral brutality, it presents a different message than the one they have been taught in school.

Howard Stevenson, who runs a program for youth called Forward Promise and Racial Empowerment Collaborative, received feedback from his participants. Many of them felt as if it does not matter how successful they become, they could still be killed by the police just for being born Black (forwardpromise.org).

The weight that people of color carry due to police brutality is too heavy a load to bear. It is even heavier for our youth.

As it stands right now, our youth do not feel safe anywhere. Research done by Taji Gibson and Janet Decker (Failure to Focus on the Discipline of Black Girls, 2019) and Shenetta Butler-Barnes and Misha Inniss-Thompson (My Teacher Doesn't Like Me: Perceptions of Teacher Discrimination and School Discipline among African American and Caribbean Black Adolescent Girls,

2020), shows the disparaging way in which Black youth are over-criminalized at school. I mention two articles of research, but there are countless others.

Black students are suspended (and expelled) at higher rates than White students for the exact same offense. Where a White student might receive an in-school suspension or detention, a Black student is given an out-of-school suspension for the same act.

This research has historically been done about Black boys, but in recent years, there has been attention paid to the disproportionate treatment of Black girls. In a school setting, the research has found that a twelve-year old White girl is seen as a child who needs to be protected (even from herself) but a twelve-year old Black girl is seen as more mature and "should know better." With that, when the twelve-year old Black girl acts out at school, the penalty is harsher because she is expected to know better.

I gave an example earlier about the nine-year old girl in Rochester, New York who was handcuffed and pepper sprayed by the police. In one officer's body camera recording, the officer is heard saying to the girl, "cut it out, you are acting like a child!" to which the nine-year old responded, "I am a child!"

This attitude exists outside of the school as well. Law enforcement officers who encounter Black youth on the streets, approach them as if they are seasoned adults. They are treated differently than White kids their age. When police officers see a group of White kids forming, they see a group of friends spending time together. The same scenario, but instead the kids are Black and are viewed as threatening and need to be neutralized.

This knowledge is known to Black youth. They start off innocent enough. We have all seen these adorable (viral) videos of little Black children walking up to the White police officer and offering some warm gesture. I recall some years ago seeing a video of a young child in a fast-food restaurant who wanted to sit at the table with the police officer. The video was well received, but surely by now that child has been exposed to a whole separate set of videos and may not be so willing to share a table with a police officer.

As a Black man who has also had a successful career in the justice system, this narrative has a harsh impact on me. I know how important it is to have a healthy respect for the law and for law enforcement officers who are trained to protect. This situation we are in is a matter of urgency for me.

As a CDI, I have a front row seat to the disproportionate way Black people are negatively impacted by the justice system. Black people are over-represented on one side of the justice system and under-represented on the other side. We must immediately change the dynamics and even the playing field. We need more

Black people in uniform; more Black people investigating crimes; more Black prosecutors and public defenders and more Black judges.

Representation matters and not to be overly dramatic, this is a life-or-death situation.

CHAPTER

Why This All Matters

As a CDI, I have a broad client base, with about 50% of my clients being Black, 40% being Hispanic and about 10% being White. It is hard not to see that the overwhelming amount of people who enter the criminal justice system are disproportionate to the demographics of the United States. In my role, I have a front row seat to the way in which people of color are arrested at higher levels.

Fortunately, in many of my cases I have been able to uncover police misconduct that has led to my clients' false entry into the criminal justice system; however, even after my investigation shows that the arrest was not a legal one, the arrest itself remains on my client's record-which can be difficult for those looking to pursue many career opportunities. Of course, there are ways to remove an arrest from someone's record, but this process is time consuming, there are fees involved, and there is no accounting for the stress and anxiety that comes along with the arrest in the first place.

I am not saying that police misconduct is present in all of my cases; however, it is my belief, based on experience, that the policies and laws that govern our judicial system are faulty, and account for the over representation of Black people and other people of color in our justice system.

The cost of an unjust system of justice is too high a price to pay, and the responsibility is falling on the shoulders of one group of people. The last few years alone have been exhausting. As soon as the community to starts to heal from one act of police brutality, another comes to light. Our society was built on a broken system. The constitution speaks of freedom but was written by men who had slaves.

We can no longer afford to continue to operate in the way that we have. We must understand that the way in which we are operating is not beneficial to anyone. Our history books speak of the African slave trade, but Africans were not the first group enslaved on American soil. The Native Americans had their land ripped from their hands; many were killed off and others were enslaved. After their numbers dwindled significantly due to intentional acts of violence or by disease, it was then that White men set sail for Africa.

What does the White man plan to do once they have killed us off or imprisoned us? What group will they go after next in order to do the work they feel is beneath them? How does killing us or imprisoning us benefit them? These are questions they are not even prepared to ask themselves, let alone answer.

They avoid true knowledge which is why there is a debate brewing about Critical Race Theory being taught in school. But it would serve students well to gain knowledge. There is an estimated 1% of people with true power in this world. Who do the 99% think will do the work of the one percenters?

Critical Race Theory is new, but its origins are not. Critical Race Theory comes from Critical Theory. Critical Theory speaks to the way the haves discriminate against the have-nots, regardless of race. A White man collecting government benefits may feel he is better than an educated Black man, but when all the Black men are killed off by police or White vigilantes, who does this benefit?

As a Black man who is educated and has experience in law enforcement, I am tasked with having this conversation. It is not always comfortable, but it is always necessary. I have often had difficulties being a Black man in this field and being able to see things through both lenses. There are days when I wear my badge and my title with pride in what I do, and then there are days when it is hard to be an officer of the court system knowing that the system can be unjust.

I do understand however that I am tasked with handling both of these roles responsibly and I also encourage other Black men and women to do the same. It is my desire to see a whole new generation of Black law enforcement officers, criminal defense investigators, and members of the judicial system.

In my first book, *Not Guilty: A Criminal Defense Investigator's Guide to Winning Your Case,* I provided in detail various tools needed to be successful in this field. In this book my goal was to show why this field is so important to maintaining our culture.

Police brutality against the Black community has been going on since the foundation of law enforcement, but just because that is the way it has always been does not mean that is the way it needs to always be.

It is time for communities of color to heal. Law enforcement agencies need to immediately stop and take a hard and introspective look at themselves, and then initiate the process of healing. The responsibility does not just lay in their hands. We have a responsibility as well. We need to go back into our communities and teach our youth. We must have dialogue, not just with our kids, but with our neighbor's kids as well. We need to go old school-get back to basics.

We must also insert ourselves into law enforcement agencies and board rooms. We need to be where decisions are being made. Pursue degrees in law and saturate our justice systems with Black attorneys and judges. This is what we can do. We must change the narrative that has been created about our community. We are not dumb and lazy; we are talented, exceptionally brilliant, and innovative.

We live in a world of "cancel culture" and I am giving us this charge; let us cancel the image that we have allowed to be portrayed on television and normalize being seen in the appropriate manner. We have played into the stereotypes for far too long, and though we have advanced despite that, imagine what we can do if we change that narrative.

When I was coming of age, young men wore their pants around their waist and had belts on. Young ladies dressed in a way that left their body to the imagination. Let us put our cell phones down and engage over genuine methods of conversation.

Let's give them more positive images of us to go viral with and less foolishness. There will always be rogue law enforcement officers and there is little we can do about that unless we position ourselves to be at the heads of policing organizations.

What I am suggesting is not hard. Black people end up at the top of whatever field we pursue. We are cut from a brilliant cloth and it is time that we are reminded.

The system that imprisons us is unjust because we have allowed it to be so for so long. We can take on the attitude of letting this ship run its own course, or we can take the helm and change the course. The choice is ours to make.

Ritualistic & Occult Crimes
April 13-16, 2015
Sunrise Police Department, Sunrise, Florida

To contact Dr. Anthony L. Robbins

Visit

Anthony L. Robbins, P.A.

Private Investigator

www.anthonylrobbins.com

CALL

(786) 490-9461

(877) 446-1264

Email: info@anthonylrobbins.com

Follow Anthony L. Robbins, P.A., Private Investigator

Ingram Content Group UK Ltd.
Milton Keynes UK
UKHW020650240723
425668UK00013B/613